7.75

D1176313

# COMING OUT FIGHTING

# Coming Out Fighting

PHILIP HOBSBAUM

> . . . leaving me desperate to pick out
> Your hands, tiny in all that air, applauding.
> PHILIP LARKIN

MACMILLAN

London . Melbourne . Toronto

1969

Published by
MACMILLAN AND CO LTD
Little Essex Street London WC2
and also at Bombay Calcutta and Madras
Macmillan South Africa (Publishers) Pty Ltd Johannesburg
The Macmillan Company of Australia Pty Ltd Melbourne
The Macmillan Company of Canada Ltd Toronto
St Martin's Press Inc New York

Printed in Great Britain by
NORTHUMBERLAND PRESS LIMITED
Gateshead

Thanks are due to the editors of the following, in which
some of these poems have appeared:
*Ambit, Encounter, Listener, New York Times, Poetry
Review, Spectator, Transatlantic Review*; and also to the
B.B.C. Third Programme.

# CONTENTS

## I

## II

## III

# IV

IN LOVING MEMORY
J.W.

# SYNOPSIS

These poems tell the story of a married man who fell in love with a girl much younger than himself. The first section records their affair, ending with the man giving up the girl who then gets married to somebody else. The second section is the Inferno of the book: a year spent in the bars and taverns of Ireland, meeting people with kindred difficulties and disappointments. The third section deals with the break-up of the man's marriage. The fourth, his re-encountering the girl — now a woman with a child and a life of her own.

I

# A LESSON IN LOVE

Sitting straightbacked, a modest Irish miss,
Knees clenched together — even then I knew
Your full mouth would open under my kiss,
The line under your eyes gave me my clue.

Now on the floor, legs thrashing your dress
Over your stocking-tops, your tight blue pants
Bursting to be off at my caress,
This is the underside of our romance.

Which is the truer? I, speaking of Donne,
Calling the act a means and not an end,
Or at your sweet pudenda, sleeking you down:
Was there no other way to be your friend?

None, none. The awkward pauses when we talk,
The literary phrases, are a lie.
It was for this your teacher ran amock:
Truth lies between your legs, and so do I.

# A SECRET SHARER

'Tell me of the house where you were born
Near Tandragee — the field, the chicken-run,
The single shop more than a mile away,
The village even farther. Make me see
You waiting while your idiot neighbour pumps,
Your youth a murmur under Tilley lamps.
Did you walk out under the clear cold stars
To where the lights of Lisburn blur the skies
Or sit over the peat fire's acrid blaze,
Hair falling carelessly about your face
And think of me, or someone not unlike?'
The picture fades into the usual dark
That keeps us separate. You have your past,
I mine, trampled to city soot and dust —
So smile, and shake your head. Our lives were such,
Spent years apart, that thoughts can barely touch,
But bodies do much better. At a nod,
Without a word, we slide into your bed
To clutch in a shared spasm. Once apart
I rise, rub myself down, bid you goodnight:
We shared a room, a bed, but not a life.
And so I leave and go home to my wife,
Whiling away in speech the hours that wane
Until my body talks to yours again.

# SILENT WORSHIP

You're gone, and now at last I feel near to you.
Your cigarette smoke still curls into the air,
The smell of you faintly lingers on my lips —
Gone, you're not quieter than when you sat cross-legged
Gazing into the fire like a basking cat —
When I spoke, did you hear me? You never said,
A nod was treasure, a murmur countless gains,
Speak to me and I'd be the king of the world.
I talk too much, I know, and about myself,
But how can you be so compact, self-contained?
Even naked it's so. I see you in the dark,
Fire on your gleaming shoulders, smile to yourself —
Yet you're not here. I speak to your presence, though,
The lingering memory of you in the room:
It doesn't reply. But neither, sweet, do you.

# THE WAITING GAME

Like a present pain
I think of that man touching you
Where I did, once.

Not so long ago
You lay back at my feet —
I eased you out of my life.

In my empty room
Your image only returns
Silent, smiling, withdrawn —

Yes, utterly withdrawn.
I wince at his hand stroking you
Where mine adventured once,

Not needing me you lie
Replete under his caress,
Burgeoning into life

While I
Locked in my childless room
Nurse my present pain.

# DIAL L FOR LEATHER

You'd never guess how many tries it took
To phone you up — how many voices spoke
Warning me off, or how every false call
Tempted the phone back on its pedestal.

Lean back and think. Suppose she isn't in?
Suppose *he* is? What if she shows concern,
Surprise, alarm? Have I the right at all
To break into a life with my phone call?

But try once more. This time a new voice spoke,
Self-confident, mature, landladylike —
Your own, it seemed. Where was that hush of breath,
That soft insinuating brogue? Gone with

Your single state, your lonely girlishness?
Many's the time I've seen you read to us
Hair tumbling over your eyes that still shone through,
Little girl lost, they thought, and only I knew

Your grunts of contentment in bed, your sudden bites,
The wild bush of hair over your secret parts:
I'd catch your eye, we'd share an inward smile,
Thinking we had deceived the world the while —

Gone with our past together, gone with the past —
I chatted, you chatted, we felt — ashes and dust,
That's what it came to, that's what I finally said.
'It's dust and ashes talking to the dead.'

# AFTERTHOUGHT

I meant to ask you—how many, how many things.
Are you happy now? Do you love him? Does it sting
Thinking of me? I ache all night after you,
Yielding to the inevitable—there I go

On about myself again. I'd like to know
All of you, all about you—I never did,
Even when intimacy seemed easiest something hid
Deep in you, down in you, past the farthest core

My body probed. And when it was time to withdraw
Something remained behind, still sacrosanct,
Untouched by me. Maybe, at last, that's why
Our love never gave birth and had to die.

# DEAD END

We once lodged in that street.
The roofs
Beetled over the kerb,
Glooming the narrow sidewalk. There
Kids kicked listlessly at stones
Between parked cars
And dogs went on their business round the steps
Where slatterns rasped.

It never offered much. Even the sun
Died on the upper windows.
                              But at the end,
Like a stone curtain shutting off
Another world, this wall.
Beyond, green tops of trees
Hinted at summer — almost we glimpsed
Gables, pinnacles, domes,
Even could guess at lawns
Sloping to tinkling streams,
Striplings at tennis, lithe girls sipping drinks . . .

For stuck
Bang in the forehead of that wall
— Where no stairs climbed, no ladder leaned —
A gate shut fast.
None of us ever saw it wide,
No one has passed right through—
For who would leave our street,
Its double banks of cars,
Sunless corners, listless kids
To peek, poke, pry
Beyond? What guarantee
Of leaves, flowering shrubs

And gardens, too, had we?
What if beyond
Stretched such another street
As ours, barren, run down?

But since we never tried the lock of that gate
To venture in
Leaving behind the world we knew
For one made new —
We never knew.

II

# A NIGHT AT LAVERY'S, LTD

I can't afford to drink, but comes the night
And shadows fall, I think of you, and straight
Go down to Lavery's, canvass the company there,
Peer through the smart of smoke and stink of beer —
Wild Bill McCulloch, Wee Mac and Ed the Ted,
Donnelly hauntedly giggling, Maguire half-dead,
Drunken old man, snuffling up Louis MacNeice
As Louis would have snuffed up Yeats had I been here
Twenty years back, drowning in golden beer.
Lavery's, memories — get the drink down! I pass
From pain to anger, from anger to bland cheer
Buying this one a round and that a round,
Giving my substance away — because I dare
Not think of you at night, I dare
Not think at night, I dare
Not think.
               Gents! please go home. Let's all go home,
Hale in synthetic friendship to *my* home,
Scoop the parcels of Guinness up from the floor,
Wobble past Lavery's paunch guarding the door,
Turn, give goodnight — Malachy's packing the room
Up, and, away with it, memory. Goodnight!
Goodnight, my soul! Goodnight, sweet world — I go
Weaving merrily home — don't think of who? —
Singing and drinking and drinking and singing. That's right;
Until next evening and the expected pain
Drive me back down to Lavery's again.

# THE RIDING-MISTRESS

You've the whip hand all right. They're driven hard
Those friends who gather round to hear you censure
Their boys, their love-lives. Conscious rectitude!
You change your hair-style, girl, but not your nature.

What of your lounge-bar yearnings after men?
You press your phone-number on each beginner,
Then sweep out smiling. But they slyly grin,
Start swopping anecdotes with one another.

You were the only girl he'd seen, one said,
Vomit and copulate at once. Another
Told how you made him tuck you up in bed.
A third called you the human vacuum cleaner.

At endless coffee-parties, late at night,
You warn your eager friends of sex and sin,
Warm, flushed and shining. Paradise without,
The observer thinks, but what a swamp within!

# A FALSE MARTYR

'It wasn't me. I wasn't there'
And then your eyes begin to shift
Searching the smoke-filled room as if
To seek aid in this questionnaire.

But no one comes. The red-haired clown
Shuffles his feet, grins by your side.
Your knowing eyes are open wide.
'It wasn't me. I'm not to blame.'

You never are. Men seize and pillage
But that's their folly, not your shame.
You fling yourself into their arms
But you were drunk. They took advantage.

More honest when your breasts fell out,
You groaned and writhed in ersatz glee.
'That awful girl? It wasn't me.'
You had the fun. Admit your fault.

# UNDERGRADUATE PARTY

Static, or nearly so, seen through the haze,
Forms slowly wheel, and, in a leisured trance,
Slowly hands grope for . . . what? Bob Dylan plays,

Christening with weazen treble each new dance:
Lank hair is fashion now, and kinky boots,
Expression wiped off each tense countenance,

As solemnly they circle, mask to mask,
Clutching for . . . Mister Tambourine Man where,
Where did you leave the curls, the moist blue eyes,

The laughter of my . . . I should not be here
And rise to leave. Nobody notices
That I'm not going to Maggie's farm no more.

# STOUT PERSON'S MEDITATION
## ON SEX

Miss Finaghy, in my General Class, eats chocolates,
Gets fatter every day, longs for a man
But goes on eating chocolates. I sympathise;
Guinness is my ruin, that and misery
Bloating and crumbling, making me want to drink more.
How did Henry VIII get on, or King Edward,
Boozed, bulky, bearded? Perhaps
It's different for men. Herbert Spencer
Decided against George Eliot on the grounds
Of general ugliness: we dream of houris,
Lissom and swift, they dream of bank balances,
Power, prestige. This grows as the bulk grows:
King Henry needed no charm, he had an axe,
A palace, followers. Maybe, at last, that's why
There's hope for me but none for Miss Finaghy.

# COCK OF THE WALK

'How ar'you? Howya doin'?' Not so well
As you, pint in one hand, fag in the other,
A beautiful virgin pulling you to bed,
Old cock of the walk. They still talk of your flights —
Chasing a Spanish lector, cheeking the Prof,
Trunk calls to London, being, at last, sent down
For robbing a pub in a glorious haze of beer,
Spirits, cigar-smoke.

                  Still, your glory dimmed,
Young acolytes hang on — brothers to those
Who in your days of grandeur dogged your wake,
Catching the girls you grandly threw away,
Drinking your bottles, your life. They're settled now,
Work in attorneys' offices, have jobs
In far-off glittering London. How about you,
Poor cock of the walk? Your plumage ruffled now,
Still holding court, still off with someone's bird,
With someone's car or flat — do I detect
A desperate tic in the rolling gleam of your eye,
That grand rich voice too Irish?

             Bulky I stand,
Bearded, myopic, amidst the ruck of the bar,
Your girls, your friends, and hear you asking me
What I can do for you, where can I get you in,
My cock of the walk, sick of the bumming life,
Taxis to Dublin, crates of Bush in the back,
Sickening bounce of glasses, bottles, cheques.
Will you at last come home to the semi-detached,
Garden, kids — all that made possible
That slap in Authority's face we so admired,

Your flout, your flourish — ask it at last to turn
The other cheek, accept your filial kiss?

I'll do it if you like — I'd rather see
You clip on your spurs for one last bloody bout,
Wreck the whole joint, tear down your father's house
In a glorious mass of plunder, wreckage, glass,
Carried out bleeding, leaving behind no hole
For cock of the walk to beat his last retreat.

# THE HARD WOMEN

Nobody wants them, they just need them, the hard women,
Big Mary, Little Mary, Angela, Carol, just sitting,
Just smoking there, beers in front of them, in a row.

Nobody'll talk to them, they just lay them, Angela,
Carol, Big Mary, Little Mary, sitting,
Not talking, just sitting, smoking in a row.

Nobody'll take them anywhere, why should they?
All they want's a man, an easy lay, some mod'd do,
Lank-haired, leather-jacketed — the kinkier the better
For Mary, Mary and Carol, in their row.

They eye me as I come in. Won't do, they think,
Married, middle-ageing, got a job, a home — they
Vet me like vultures, I walk under the eye
Of Mary, Mary and Carol in their row.

What could I say to them, even if I tried. Those four —
Large cheerful tart, small withdrawn whore, tough girl
Narrowly watching, expert at soixante-neuf —
Talk's not their line, nor books. Not even drink
For Big Mary, Little Mary, Carol, Angela, sitting.

Their one question — 'where's the party?' So they sit,
Whiling away till closing time, when some
Rancid tenement, rank bedsitter, will bear
Their brusque incursion, vulture shrieks, descending
Like hordes on bodies, picking at bitter scrub —

'Hi Mary,' 'Hi Mary — Angela — Carol'. Hi,
And into bed, and out of bed next day,
Still hard, still seeking, those women, night after night,
The Maries, and Carol, and Angela, in their row.

# UP SHIT CREEK

Doctor Malfonte is testing the maid for cancer,
His degree's in theology. Over his head
Vince is being sucked off by a well-known bang
He's too fastidious to shag. Generally speaking
The town's quiet at this time of the year,
Except Big Stinko fixing a fuse to a fire
He means to throw at Balmoral. Shuffling in
Old Tom lights the bar up — he's had his annual bath,
Grottmann enjoys the sunlight fingering his Monk
Pretending it's Sylvia Webb. Given over to vice?
Come out to the alley, Sally's being had by a mod,
The fifty-seventh this year. In experience,
Quantitatively speaking, she's got us beat.
Just up the road Rosalind's leaving home
With a random selection of kids. They say he drinks,
He says it's because she leaves home. On a desk
In the Language Department back a hired help
Is screwing our Yankee research girl. Down below
DeJong smugs at the wall, doing damn all
For four thousand a year — the typist suffers instead.
Over in the quad the students spread on the lawn
Are groping each other again — some pretend to read.
Fran walks on the other side — seldom seen out
Except with two priests to protect him from the flesh
So abundantly displayed. Those mini-skirts,
Conventional knickers under the op-art gear,
Big boots, big knees, big thighs — those topless tops,
Revealing towers of Ilium, those jeans,
Bums sticking out criss-crossed with garter-belts,
Christ, what they do to me! Every year's a rape,
This time next year it'll be Uncle in the dock —
He doesn't even care. He'll burn and burn,
Feeling his nerves like telegraphs or a chart

In the Anatomy Lab., till, send the fog,
He'll shuffle through the night, spit like Old Tom,
Smell like Big Stinko, drink like Ed the Ted,
Be found in the drain next morning, sloshed to the skies,
Wet as a rag, and dying. This happy thought
Is all that stops him reaching for knock-out drops;
He writes it down instead. O.K.? God bless.

# BLACK BENNY SOLILOQUISES

Oh, sure, like, I seen 'em all come in here —
Professors, like, an' poets an' artists all givin' themselves airs —
I can give them the air, don't you worry now. All the same —
Start 'em on culture an' the like o' that, after a few they're
        down to it —
Women. All the same, ever' single one o' them. Ye never
See 'em wi their wives, no, they're home watching telly, and
        wi'out them
— D'ye see my meanin' — the men are all unprotected, like.
Well here I am with, like, my harem as ye might say —
All right for student fellers, the like o' those,
But married men wi' families — it's not right, I'm tellin' ye.
Last week we had a feller in — what was his name? a clergyman
        they say, he was once,
Ran off with one of his parishioners' wives. Cunt-happy. That's
        them, I'm tellin' ye —
I had him in here the other day, afloat, he was, pissed to the
        kidneys,
Cussin' and blindin', in my bar. Right, I said, that's it, you're
        barred —
I mean it, he'll stay barred, I don't care who he is, I don't care
        what he's done,
They come to my bar an' they drink an' use foul language.
        Now I'll not have that,
No, not if it was — what d'ye call him? — Shakespeare, like,
        or that feller Yeats,
Nobody comes cussin' and blindin' in my bar.

'After twenty-seven the only kicks you get
Are in the teeth,' said Ed the Ted. 'I
Miss your little thing. You, too' wrote Clare
To Hendy. 'Sure, only a bastard
Would spoil a bloke's Saturday night' snarled Little Mac
Sweating with anger. 'You don't
Crap on your own hearthrug' said Leslie, said Vince
'Don't come the intellect, tell 'em you're the janitor,'
      said Raikes
'I suppose I shall have to tie a knot in it.'

                       My friends,
Co-habitants of hell, I deserve your company:
My enemy's enemy, too, should have such friends.

# A LONELY MAN

He potters round his flat, Mozart his friend
Speaking from Hi-Fi systems, carefully removes
Mud from his Tintawn inconsiderate pals
Brought in, with bottles, after the pubs closed —
'O that's all right' he'll bellow, glaring cheerfully
Over his modish spectacles — presses his trousers
Fashioned from Soho for someone else's wedding
On that same carpet with a special iron
That steams and heats and smooths. Once I cut my fingers
Using his super-hollow-ground carving knife
Only to be solaced by extra-luxury plaster
Guaranteed washable. Even his french-letters
Are of the best.

                    Dear Raikes,
So gruff and so indomitable, only she
Who loved you best could know you. Most generous of men
Doubting my solvency, cheques all stopped, you said
'I have an account with the Belfast Savings Bank,
How much can I lend you?' — we wish you all
You've not the selfishness to wish yourself:
So that maybe in years to come I'll see you
Not pottering lonely in that tasteful flat
Where stereo works but taps, alas, do not,
Which doesn't possess a teapot — no, but, say
Playing with babies on a sunny lawn
Watched by a happy girl who returns your love
As we, with the best will ever, never can.

# LAVERY'S LAST GOOD NIGHT
## For Paddy Lynch

Nobody comes here unless there's something wrong with them.
I look around
That semi-circular room hung with pop-art,
Those groups of chairs round tables
And the people
Who make the place — the tarts set in their row,
Big Jim rescuing Sully, and Drunken Jim
Weeping into his vodka, Malachy
Weaving swiftly between tables to sort out
Some con that Donnelly has put
On a new soft touch — 'sure it wasn't me, Malachy,'
He'll protest half-laughing, 'sure you know me' — we do;
And you, you bastard, ambulant barrel of stout,
Hair to your greasy shoulders, one ear-ring,
Patron saint of this place — why are *you* liked?
Benny expels you, Lavery gets you back:
Once you came in with twopence, sat all day
With a glass of orange, we idiots poured gin in
So that your fat red face burst out
In pustules — 'a secret weapon,' Eddy said.
Once you stood up blind drunk and raved to God
To prove himself by striking you. Wisely He didn't,
And on one fatal night
How you came in, face beaming, 'Drinks all round,
Malachy, make them doubles, Kennedy's shot.'
I have seen you sign a cheque for ten bob on a beer-mat
(The bank cashed it, they thought it was a joke)
Or spend a hundred and fifty quid in a night
(Oh, Lavery's filled up that time) drinking yourself
Half pints of pernod — you fell downstairs, you bum,
And thought you were flying.
When two or three of your friends are gathered together

In Belfast, Dublin, Glasgow or the Smoke
There you are also living your impossible life
Over again in our talk —
'Do you remember
How Lynch wore a shirt for fifteen weeks and a half
Until it disintegrated? Do you remember
How Carolyn and Doherty tore off his horrible clothes
And threw him in a bath? Do you remember
How, penniless again, Lynch went around
To every stranger (the regulars knew him too well)
With an empty glass, solemnly saying "Karl Marx:
To each according to his need"?' What you most need
Is happenings. 'Run your hand up her thigh, she'll love it,'
You'll urge, or else you'll casually throw a glass
Not caring where it'll land, or give a girl
Someone else's bottle of Scotch to drink
And have her off in a toilet while Wild Bill roars
'Where is that Lynch? I'll Lynch the fucking bastard,
He's got my dolly'—how many lying references
I've written you, you crud, but this one's true:
Or as Raikes said, looking round a Lynch-less bar
— You'd bummed off to London, or Paris, or Hong Kong—
'There's nothing to be said in his favour, nothing at all,
Except that the bastard doesn't let things get dull.'

# III

## THE ICE SKATERS

They merrily weave over the blue transparency,
Fir trees against snow-threatening sky etched
Nicely in, curvet, chassée, and slide

Merrily off — a long take, this time. I see them
Shining blonde and lustrous dark and honey —
coloured meet, escape, pirouette, and off again

Over the smooth hard sheen. Under their legs
Twirling so merrily what deep acres live
Of dark or weed or slow fish nudging past,

What bottom-sods of mud, what tangles of weed —
They slide over the surface, beckoning us on,
Gingerly we follow, test the security — fine,

They call, weaving away merrily. You
Venture to catch them up, reach out, and
Find yourself struggling in dirty water. Call,

Ice in your mouth, spluttering blindly, down,
Down into the mud, entangling with weed you go.
Their laughter tinkles prettily over the ice.

# DREAM CHILDREN

I had this dream. We were all drinking together,
But I was watching the time — you had to go home,
All of you, out of the fug, into your beds
Clean and white, the healthy wakening, work.
So rang for a taxi, talked hard to get you in.
One said she'd stop for another, another had a friend
She ought to pick up, a third — well, that third got lost,
I searched like a maniac for her, forced in the rest.
We started. Oh, what a route! Up hilly streets,
Past derelict shops, blind windows, holes in the wall,
We rattled and groaned. What detours! 'Where are we now?'
I'd yell, peering through crusted glass to the night
Solidly banked beyond. We trundled still —
You chattered, she chattered, we stopped, we started—some-
        one
Whoever it was, had a bottle. We drank some more:
I woke up sweating. Never, it seemed, would we
Find our way home, you lost in the night,
Boozing and sleeping around, I locked in my head,
Seeking and seeking for what I shall never have.

# COSTUME JEWELLERY

The first time I took you out tiny pagodas
Swung from your ears,
But, kissing you goodnight, one brushed off,
Rolled away, disappeared.

You laughed it off, went home, went to sleep.
Half the night through
I wandered up and down that alley
Searching, for you.

There was that pearl ring, too, I remember
— Pearls are for tears
They said when we got engaged.
And, with the years

Those pearls fell down, rolled off,
Or withered dry.
You yourself tired of the trinket
Stowed it away.

Where is it now? Mislaid, stolen,
Nobody cares,
Bunched with forgotten things,
Dried with your tears,

Dried with our lives together.
What of our marriage?
Gone with the trinkets, dear,
Gone with the pearls and tears,
Pillaged, disparaged.

# HOUSE OF SAND

We knew it wouldn't last. That's why
We thumbed in turrets so prettily, fashioned doors
And windows, too, for small sand people to come

In and go out again — our little house,
Dark damp sand, driveway scored in, the sea
Encroaching upon our play.

                              We watched it fall,
Prey to grey water swirling, helped it on
With a good boot or two, stood by and smiled —

Our house of sand melts to a shapeless mound.

# THE SICK LION

retreats to his hidden fastnesses to lick
his bleeding paws, blink vengefully at the gloom,
sullen and unconsoled. All night
the forest is shaken by profound complaints,
growling, reverberant. Lesser denizens
creep about twilight tasks assigned to fear,
hope unobtrusively. The other beasts
keep well away, scenting the sickness, leave
him to his waking pain. Until the day,
sinews sewn up, torn ligaments healed, he leaps
out in a blaze of thunder, tears the bush
clean from the earth, lays waste the pest of fowls,
jackals, camp-followers. That will be the day
when all find themselves judged for their detachment,
when the jungle, at last, assumes its rightful name.

IV

# HEART'S JOURNEY

How many times I caught sight of your face
Looking away, how many weary days
Tracking you down through endless trodden ways?

Did you go round that corner? When I looked
Only the long street stretched, level and bare,
So many days I searched, so many ways.

Were you the one, poised to alight, who fled
Seeing my glance? Or, in the window caught,
Half-turned away, it seemed, away always?

Or could it be this: imprinted in my brain
Always you flee my path like a shadow lost
Down trodden ways through my downtrodden days?

Do what you will, flit when you may, in shade
Or subtle moonlight, know I seek you out
Day after day through all these dreary ways,

Trusting, at last, to meet you face to face,
Sure touch of hand, pressure of lip, to end
My journey through so many ways and days.

I saw you, a grave young Madonna at the gate.
My heart went out
Greeting your tender heart — for two long years
Dear, my beloved, we have trod on love,
Beaten it, crushed it, crucified it, and
Here we walk together — the happiest day
For two long years.
We wander through that ever so public park
Seeking a place to feed your child, we sit
Finally down on damp grass, two nuns pass by
— Who cares? — the park keeper watches us
With deep suspicion, a honeymoon couple with
Another man's child — who cares, who cares, who cares.
It came on to rain, it stopped, I didn't care.
There was a tedious bus — I didn't care —
Laden with schoolboys who gibbered as we got off
So incongruously young — I didn't care —
You with your hair now greying, dear, I
Paunched and bespectacled. When the time comes,
As come it will, we'll shed these saddened years,
Leap into each other's arms like kids again,
Till then,
Greetings, Madonna of the garden gate,
My heart's gone out.

# THE THIEF OF LOVE

I stole into your house, became
The thief of love,
Saw how the cluttered kitchen, bare board floor
Littered with baby-things, the wooden settle
On which I sat — you warned me off, said
'There's a cup of milk beside you' — told of home,
Your home, and his, not mine. I didn't care,
I didn't care, I didn't care. I sat
Smoking and watching you smoke, came over and
Stroked your poor aching head, said goodbye, went
With no more fuss than just a good friend makes
Bidding adieux, and yet
I left with a full burden. I had become
The thief of love.

'You can't put back the clock' — and your commands
Are sacred. But, dear, clocks, like us, have hands.

# COMING OUT FIGHTING

'I hope when the fighting starts you'll be by my side
On the barricades' I told my friend. He said
'It depends what the fighting's about.' What the fighting's
        about?
Fighting is about fighting, the crunch is about the crunch,
War about war — all that matters is
Who's by your side on the barricades.
                              So,
Seeing you, love, plumped out with bearing your child,
Sagging with the years of sorrow, new tired lines
Etched in that trusting face, I look at you
Knowing there are so many beautiful girls in the world,
Younger than you, and slimmer, nicer to know —
And give them up. Love isn't looks or grace,
Not cars or villas, not night flights to Madrid —
I'd rather lay my pudgy hand on yours,
Stained, now, and work-worn, than lay whoever you like—
Bardot, La Lollo, Loren. I see now
What always looked me straight in the face, so
Trustfully, love, trustfully, love, love
Is about love.

# BREAKING UP

Those two sad sentences toll in my ears:
'I have been here before' and
'I shall not pass this way again'.

                                   Fear not,
Beloved, what is whole stays whole,
I'll not tear down your house, it rots itself
With trivial decay. I know, I have
Been here before. I know what it is to live,
To love, even, and row. The smallest thing
Grates on your nerves — whatever he does is wrong —
Bringing you breakfast in bed, cooking a steak,
Shopping, taking the kid out. It's so wrong,
So trivially so. Almost you'd rather he
Fought you, attacked you, gave you some excuse
For hating him. You don't. No row
Is ever won. Suppose you shout him down,
You've hurt the one being that cares for you
Dearer than all the world, suppose he wins,
You've lost again, and he's gained nothing but hurt
For having hurt you. I
Know, dearest, I have been this way before.
I know what it is to see my dear one's eyes
Mirror with tears, to wrangle a night through
Seeking a way back to a shared embrace,
To kill the thing I love. To love so much
That I relinquish, let her go. And you,
My dearer love, so waited for, think this —
I pull down no man's house, I wreck no life,
Only when by sadness and slow attrition you
Find you can bear his pain no longer, dear,
Let him, as I did, go. I have been there before,
And I shall never pass that way again.

# WATCHING AND WAITING

Why do I sit so chastely by your side
In this lone field, not tumble you, not slide
Ever so gently my hand up your bare thigh?
Because I live in hope. There is no doubt,
No doubt at all that one day your dear
Eyes will search into mine and find their peace.
Therefore I live in hope. The smallest touch,
Whiff of a shared cigarette, is more to me
Than nine years' broken marriage. I can wait,
Wait in the cold, in the dark, warm myself
At the flames of my hope. And should it come to pass
That this hope, too, proves futile, and in hell
I lie consumed with passion, even then,
As poets say the damned do, I will slake
My scorched eyes on that heaven divorced from me
And live, as now, in hope.

She hums listlessly about her chores —
Will the plates never get washed? and when they are
More plates to wash again — listens out
For the baby's fitful cry — tidying up,
Pauses, strokes back her hair, looks around chaos
And thinks of him —
That dream that never was, that might-have-been,
Voice in the wilderness, touch in the night. Remembers
The stolen days together, years back, how many —
'I was an adolescent then,' she muses but
Catches in the mirror her secret smile, the one
Her husband never sees, that lights her eyes,
Dulled, normally, to household chores. And again,
With an unconscious sigh, she sets to, tries
— Listlessly, too listlessly — to set
Chairs in some rightful order, wipes up milk
The baby slopped, removes paint
('That'll be our dining-room when it's finished')
Into a cupboard already packed, and waits
For husband to come home.
                                        Alone all day,
Stuck in the wilderness, her and her child, she looks
Aimlessly out at the hills. Afternoons, sometimes,
Wheels out her child or takes her in a sling
Like a young gipsy over the grassy slopes —
That's sometimes. Sometimes it rains,
Sometimes she just sits down amid the things
Littering the floor, abstractedly takes a pen
From the baby's jaws — 'Now Katey, will y' behave' —
Does nothing. Minutes it seems to her. Mike's car
Growls in the distance, assures her it's really hours.
                                        Then he comes home,
Nothing prepared, nothing really done,

And 'Christ, I'm tired,' he'll say, and sit in his chair
And pick up the paper, interlude before TV.
What's he done? Who's he spoken to, or seen?
She doesn't know. But in the flickering light
When he is staring into a shadow world
She has her dream-world, too, and thinks of him,
That other, whom she had and did not keep,
Remembering the brush of his hand along her spine,
Remembering his tongue on her stomach, slide of thighs,
Remembering. And then she glows again,
And finds somewhere to go.